The Heroic

Hatimtai

Compiled by Mrs Rungeen Singh

Young Learner Publications™
G-1 Rattan Jyoti
18 Rajendra Place
New Delhi -110008 (INDIA)
Ph.: 25750801, 25820556
Fax: 91-11-25764396

Printed at : Kumar Offset Printers, Delhi-110092

CONTENTS

THE BIRTH OF HATIMTAI

The rich King of Yemen was a good ruler. He looked after his people very well and his people loved him. Yet he was sad because he had no children.

The unhappy king often said to his wife, "We have everything. God has given us fame and money, yet we are not happy because we don't have a child."

The king and the queen prayed to God every day. Then one day, one of the queen's maids came running to the king. She told him that the queen was soon going to become a mother. The king was overjoyed on hearing the good news.

He took off his costly necklace and gave it to the queen's maid as a reward for bringing the good news.

After a few months, the queen gave birth to a son. The king was extremely happy.

The baby boy was very cute and sweet. The king loved to hold him in his arms.

He told all his people to celebrate the birth of his son, who would be the ruler of Yemen after him.

The baby prince was named Hatimtai. For a whole week, all the people celebrated the birth of Prince Hatimtai.

The king thanked God for blessing them with a child. He distributed lots of money and gifts to the needy people in his kingdom.

Everybody was happy. The king then called some fortune-tellers to foretell the future of the newborn baby.

They said that Hatim would grow up to be a tall, handsome and brave man. People would love him, and he would be famous all over the world for his kindness.

This made the king very happy, and he rewarded those fortune-tellers with gifts and money.

The king ordered his courtiers, "Tell the people of Yemen to send all the boys born on the same day as Prince Hatimtai to the palace. These boys will be brought up like princes in the palace along with Hatim."

The people of Yemen were very excited when they heard this news.

All the parents were happy that their sons would be brought up in the royal palace as princes.

They started coming to the palace one after the other with their sons.

When the courtiers began counting the babies, they found that six thousand more boys had been born on the same day as Hatimtai.

All the six thousand boys were to be brought up in the palace.

Each child was to be looked after by a separate nurse, so many nurses were appointed to look after Prince Hatimtai and those six thousand boys.

There was a lot of confusion when so many baby boys were brought to the palace.

All the people became busy in making the babies comfortable in the palace.

The cries of those six thousand babies filled the palace, and this made the king and the queen very happy.

The king and the queen thought that till Prince Hatimtai was born, they could not hear the cry of a single child, and now they could hear the cries and gurgles of so many children in the palace.

THE KIND BABY

At night, while almost all the babies were comfortably settled, a few babies were still crying.

Even Prince Hatimtai had not taken milk. Everyone including the queen tried to feed him, but he did not drink a single drop of milk.

This made the king and the queen very worried.

The anxious queen started crying. She was afraid that something wrong might happen to the baby, as he was not drinking milk.

Someone advised the king, "My Lord, there is a wise holy man who can help us with this problem."

The holy man was respectfully invited to the palace. When he came, the king welcomed him.

The king then asked the holy man, "Why is my son not having milk? Is everything fine with him? I am very worried about him."

The holy man said, "Don't worry, my son. This just shows that your prince is very kind."

The king did not understand anything. He gave the holy man a confused look.

The holy man asked, "Are there more babies in your palace?"

The king said, "Yes, there are six thousand male babies in the palace."

The holy man said, "Your kind son will have milk only when all the other children have been given their feed."

The king immediately shouted, "Go and check if the other boys have had milk."

One servant said, "Some babies have not yet been fed, My Lord."

The king ordered the nurses to feed the babies at once.

When all the babies had been fed, baby Hatim began to drink milk.

All the people were surprised to see the sensitivity of baby Hatim. Even as a child, he could feel the pain and discomfort of others.

The people of Yemen praised Prince Hatim for his kind nature.

The holy man blessed Hatim and told the king that he would grow up to be a very kind person.

HATIM AS A KING

Hatimtai grew up to be a tall and handsome teenager. He mastered all kinds of fighting skills.

All the six thousand boys, who grew up in the palace with Prince Hatim, were also given training in warfare. They too became skilled fighters.

Since all the boys had been brought up together, they had become very good friends. They were very loyal to Prince Hatim. If he faced any problem, all the boys helped him out of it.

Once a prince of a neighbouring kingdom came to the palace. The prince's father had come to meet Prince Hatim's father for some work.

The prince of the neighbouring kingdom was very proud and spoke to the six thousand boys, in Hatim's palace, in a disrespectful and insulting manner.

Hatim asked the prince to be polite to the boys because he considered them as his brothers.

The prince started laughing at Hatim. Seeing this, all the six thousand boys came and stood around Hatim ready to fight for him.

Hatim told his brothers not to say anything. But when the prince insulted Hatim again and called him a coward, the prince found himself surrounded by all the six thousand boys, looking at him angrily.

The proud prince got afraid and stopped laughing. It was only when Hatim asked his brothers to forgive the prince did they leave him. Seeing himself free, the prince quickly ran away and sat next to his father.

Everyone in the court praised this unity among the boys. They admired the fact that all the six thousand boys loved each other.

When Hatim was only twelve years old, his father died. The death of the king left the entire kingdom grief-stricken. The people lamented the death of their kind-hearted king.

During that time, Hatim was learning the finer nuances of looking after the kingdom.

Some trusted ministers looked after the kingdom until Hatim was ready to become the king.

Then at the age of fourteen, Hatim was crowned as the King of Yemen. He was kinder than his father. Every needy person in his kingdom was allowed to walk up to the palace to ask for money.

The poor and the needy could come to ask for help at any time of the day.

Even after becoming the king, Hatim maintained his brotherly relation with the six thousand boys in the palace.

They were given important jobs in the kingdom, and they helped Hatim in the administration of the kingdom.

He helped them when they were in trouble. If they asked for anything, Hatim never refused them. He made sure that all of them were happy.

When they grew up, they were married to the girls of their choice. Even their families were well looked after.

HATIM AND THE LION

The animals in Hatimtai's kingdom were well looked after.

Hatim would often go to the forest but not for hunting down the animals. He would check on the animals to ensure that they were healthy and had enough to eat.

If an animal was ill, it was taken to the palace for treatment and then it was again released into the forest.

Hatim was so sensitive to the pain of others that he didn't allow the butchering of any innocent animal in his kingdom.

Once, he was passing through a dense forest with his men. Suddenly, a lion, with a ferocious look on his face, came and stood in front of Hatim.

Hatim's troop was scared and wanted to run away for life. But Hatim, to the great surprise of everyone, got off his horse and walked towards the lion.

The immense benevolence of his soul gave him the ability to see the good of others even if it was at the cost of his own life.

The humane and courageous Hatim went straight to the lion and looked at it with kindness.

He said to the lion, "You must be hungry. I am right, am I not? You have got nothing to eat, so you must be angry too."

The lion looked at Hatim as if it understood all that Hatim was saying.

The lion stood still as Hatim spoke on, "You can eat us all if you want because if you are hungry you have the right to eat us."

Slowly the lion's expression changed, and it looked at Hatim with respect. The cruelty on its face faded away as it heard Hatim's kind words.

Hatim said, "You are a creation of God, and you get your food by hunting."

The people wanted to stop Hatim from going closer to the lion, but they knew that nobody could stop him from doing what his kind heart told him to do.

He sat in front of the iion with a heart that had no fear but only compassion for the lion.

He said, "You can eat us all but please spare our horses, as I don't like animals being killed."

The lion looked at Hatim, turned around and walked away.

All the people with Hatim were astonished to see the effect of Hatim's words on the lion.

They went back and told everyone about this strange encounter with the lion. Hatim was praised by all for his brave and compassionate heart .

THE POOR MAN

Everyone liked Hatimtai for his kindness. He made sure that no one went hungry in his kingdom.

One day, he was riding through a forest when he heard a small child crying. He stopped to see from where the voice was coming. He got off his horse and walked towards the direction from where the voice was coming.

He saw a hut in which a man was sitting with his wife and child. It was this child who was crying.

Hatim asked them, "Why is this child crying?"

The mother replied, "The child is crying because he is hungry and we have no food to feed him."

"Why don't you have food to feed the child?" asked Hatim.

The father said, "I am a poor woodcutter. Today I fell down from a tree and hurt myself, so I could not go to cut wood."

Hatim took out some gold coins and told the poor man to take the money and buy some food for his child. But the woodcutter stood up, folded his hands and said, "I know that you are a kind king, but I can't take anything from you."

Hatim was surprised to hear the woodcutter's reply.

He asked, "Why can't you take this money? I am your king, and it is my duty to help you."

"If I take this money, I would feel as if I have got alms from you. I don't want to beg for money. I don't want my family to live on charity," said the woodcutter.

"But you did not beg for money. I was the one who asked you to take it," said Hatim.

"I am sorry, but I take money only when I have worked hard for it," said the woodcutter.

Hatim did not say anything for sometime. The woodcutter thought that Hatim was offended by his refusal to take the money. But Hatim was not angry with the woodcutter.

With a smile on his face, he said, "People say that I am kind and good, but I think that you are better than me."

"What are you saying, My Lord? I am just a simple poor man," said the woodcutter.

"No, you are truly great. Your child is crying, yet you don't want to take money that you have not worked for. God bless you! I will never forget you," said Hatim.

Later, Hatim offered him work in his palace and paid a handsome salary to him.

HELPING THE FOX

Once Hatim had gone to a forest. On his way back to the palace, he heard a pitiful cry of an animal.

Hatim stopped his horse and got down to see which animal was crying.

He saw a vixen crying, "Oh, my husband! Oh God, save him!"

Hatim compassionately looked at the vixen. She had her four children with her.

He asked her, "What is the matter? Why are you crying?"

The vixen said, "My husband, the fox, has been caught by a hunter. The hunter will kill my husband. What should I do?"

"Don't worry. I will get your husband back from the hunter," said Hatim, and he went to the house of the hunter.

He said, "I need the blood of a fox or a wolf to cure someone. Do you hunt foxes and wolves?"

The hunter replied, "Yes, today I have caught a fox. Would you like to buy it for five gold coins?"

"Yes," said Hatim and gave the money to the hunter. However, before leaving he warned the hunter, "Take these gold coins and give me the fox. But next time if you hunt animals, I will not spare you."

The hunter took the money and set the fox free.

Hatim and the fox walked to the place where he had seen the vixen crying.

The four children and the vixen welcomed the fox with a lot of love.

Hatim felt very nice that he had given so much joy to this family. But suddenly the fox fainted and fell down.

Hatim ran and brought some water for the fox from a nearby pond.

The vixen said, “No, water will not help. Only a human’s blood can cure him.”

At once, Hatim cut a vein of his hand.

The vixen shouted, “What are you doing? Don’t cut yourself.”

“Hush! We have to get your husband well again. If my blood can recover him, I’ll be more than happy,” said Hatim.

Blood came out from the cut, and Hatim let the blood fall into the mouth of the fox.

The fox soon recovered.

The vixen thanked Hatim for saving her husband's life.

The fox said, “You have a heart of gold. I have seen no man with so much compassion for animals. May God bless you!”

When the children thanked Hatim for saving their father’s life, he said, “You are welcome. As a king, it is my duty to take care of all the creatures of my kingdom.”

After this, Hatim took leave from the fox and his family.

On seeing Hatim going back, the children got worried and innocently asked, "What if the hunter comes back to catch our father again? What will we do then?"

Hatim replied in a kind voice, "The hunter will never trouble you again. You need not worry. Now I have to go. Goodbye."

Bidding farewell to Hatim, the vixen said, "Goodbye! May the Almighty protect you in all your endeavours."

This was yet another incident where Hatim helped someone in trouble, without considering the pain he himself had to undergo.

MUNEER SHAH

One day while taking rounds of his city, Hatimtai rode very fast and his horsemen were left behind.

He entered the forest and saw a man sitting under a tree. The man looked like a beggar. He had torn clothes and thorns on his feet. He looked very sad.

Hatim felt sorry for the young man. He went closer and noticed that although his clothes were torn, he seemed to belong to a good family.

Hatim asked, "Who are you, brother? Why are you in such a bad state?"

The man said, "I am Muneer Shah. I am sad because life seems useless to me and the hope of happiness in life is lost to me."

Hatim said, "Be brave! Come with me to my palace, and tell me your story."

Muneer asked, "Who are you?"

He said, "I am Hatimtai, the King of Yemen. But tell me what is this that you are holding?"

"This is the portrait of Husn Bano, the woman I love," said Muneer.

Hatim again asked Muneer to come to his palace. Muneer agreed and went with him.

In Hatim's palace, Muneer was well looked after. When he had taken bath and had put on fine clothes, he was provided with a good dinner.

When Hatim asked him to narrate his story, Muneer Shah said, "I am the Prince of Sham. I heard of Husn Bano, a beautiful young woman, and I wanted to see her. I knew that I would not be allowed to go to her palace, so I called an artist. I gave him money and told him to paint a portrait of Husn Bano so that I could see how she looked like."

"The artist agreed to go to Husn Bano's city and paint her portrait."

"I arranged for him to reach her city safely. He went there and stayed in a guest house."

"There he came to know that Husn Bano did not meet strangers. He realised that it would not be possible to make her painting."

"He then sent a message to her that he had something to say that only she should hear. His trick worked, and she agreed to meet him."

"When he went to meet her, she came and sat behind a curtain. My generous and kind-hearted Husn Bano told the artist to ask for anything that he needed and promised that she would provide it for him."

"Imagine Hatim, how bounteous and amiable my Husn Bano is!" said Muneer as he looked admiringly at the portrait of Husn Bano.

"Yes, she does seem to be a kind-hearted woman," said Hatim.

He further added, "She is beautiful too as can be seen from the portrait."

"It's not only her outer beauty, but also her inner beauty which has captured my heart and soul. I really love her," said Muneer, with eyes full of love for Husn Bano.

"Muneer, I can clearly see how dearly you love her," said Hatim.

Then Hatim asked, "You have the portrait with you. How did the artist manage to paint her portrait when she was not ready to meet anyone?"

Muneer explained, "The artist was a clever fellow. He requested her to allow him to make a portrait of her without meeting him."

"He told Husn Bano that she could sit in her balcony, and he would sit on the road outside. He would keep a wide pot of water and see her face in it, and then he would paint her portrait."

"Husn Bano was so impressed with his clever plan that she agreed. She allowed him to make her portrait."

"As was planned, Husn Bano sat behind a curtain and the artist painted her portrait seeing her reflection in the water of the pot kept in front of her."

"The clever artist made two portraits. One he gave to Husn Bano and the other he gave to me."

"The first time when the artist showed me this portrait, I could not take my eyes away from it. I fell in love with her and decided to marry her."

"I rushed to my parents and told them that I was going to meet her at once. They were not happy with my decision. They wanted me to marry another girl, but I could only think of Husn Bano."

MUNEER AND HUSN BANO

Muneer continued, "I told my parents that I loved Husn Bano and would marry only her. After much persuasion and pleading, they allowed me to go and meet Husn Bano."

"I rushed to her city as soon as I could. I was so excited to meet her that I did not even think about from where to go. I crossed deserts, forests and swam through rivers, but I did not mind anything. I just wanted to see my Husn Bano and nothing else mattered."

"After listening to you, I feel people are right when they say that love drives one crazy," said Hatim laughingly.

"Once you fall in love, dear Hatim, only then shall you know of a lover's throes," said Muneer smilingly.

Then Muneer continued with his story, "I reached Husn Bano's city with a lot of hope. The desire to meet the girl of whom I had dreamt day and night was immense."

"As I was over exhausted and had not eaten anything for a few days, I had become very weak."

"At the gates of the city, I nearly fell on the ground. The guards carried me to a nice rest house. There I refused to eat anything till I was taken to meet Husn Bano."

"They then took me to her. When I went inside, she was sitting behind a curtain."

"So I could not see her. She spoke to me. Her voice was so sweet that I forgot all my pain and quietly sat listening to her. She requested me to eat something as she didn't want anybody in her city to be hungry."

"Then I told her that I was not a beggar but a prince, and I had come to her city after facing a lot of hardships. Finally I told her that I wanted to marry her because I loved her."

"It was then that she told me about the seven puzzles that a man who desires to marry her needs to solve. She clearly told me that she will marry me only if I solve all the seven puzzles."

"What did you do then?" asked Hatim.

Muneer said, "Hatim, I could not understand any of the puzzles so I moved out of her palace. It was with a hopeless state of mind that I entered the forest. It was then that you found me and brought me to your palace."

Hatim said, "What are the seven puzzles that you have to solve?"

Muneer said, "The first thing that I have to find out is that who said these words, 'Have seen it once, but would like to see it again.' I also have to find out why these words were said."

HUSN BANO

Hatimtai asked, "Who is Husn Bano? Tell me something about her."

Muneer said that an old man had told him about her. Husn Bano was the only daughter of a rich merchant. When he fell fatally sick, he called the king, who was his friend, and requested him to look after his daughter.

He gave all his wealth to the king. This wealth was to be given to Husn Bano when she grew up.

The king looked after Husn Bano very well. When she grew up, the king gave her a small palace and all her wealth, and she comfortably lived there.

Husn Bano's nurse, who had always been with her, was like a mother to her.

Once her nurse told her that now that she was old enough to marry, many bad people may desire to marry her in greed for her wealth.

So the nurse decided to put a condition for anyone who wanted to marry Husn Bano. A set of seven puzzles had to be solved by the one who wished to marry her. She wrote these seven puzzles on the wall of the palace for everyone to know.

Muneer told Hatim, "Out of the seven puzzles the first four are to find out who said these words and why."

"The first is, 'Have seen it once but would like to see it again.'"

"The second is, 'Do good and cast it into the river.'"

"The third is, 'Evil begets evil.'"

"The fourth is, 'Pleasure lies in speaking the truth.'"

"The fifth is to get information about the mountain that echoes."

"The sixth is to get the pearl that is equal to the size of a duck's egg."

"The seventh is to gather information about the Hammam Baadgard."

Hatim said, "These seven puzzles are not easy."

Muneer said, “I know. That is why no one has come to try out these seven puzzles. But what will I do, Hatim? I love Husn Bano, and I want to marry her. But how can I solve these seven puzzles?”

THE HOLY MAN

Muneer told Hatim that Husn Bano lived all alone in her palace with only an old nurse and a few guards to look after her. Once she had been caught in a serious trouble.

Once, a holy man came to Husn Bano's city. She asked her nurse to call the holy man to her palace for dinner.

The holy man came and was well looked after by Husn Bano herself.

The forty students of the holy man were also served dinner by the servants.

After the dinner, the holy man asked for Husn Bano's permission to leave with his disciples.

Before he left, Husn Bano offered him some costly gifts but he refused saying, "What attachment do men like us have with wealth?"

The holy man was actually a robber and the forty students with him were robbers too.

These robbers used to disguise themselves as holy men and then gain entry into the houses of rich people. They used to see the costly things of a particular house during the day, and at night they used to steal away everything.

That night the holy man and his men came to steal valuables from Husn Bano's palace.

At midnight when all was quiet, Husn Bano heard some noise. She woke up and saw a band of robbers stealing her wealth.

She recognised the chief robber. He was none other than the man who had disguised himself as a holy man. Her servants tried to stop the robber, but they were overpowered by the robbers.

Next morning, Husn Bano went to the king to inform him about the holy man who was actually a robber. But the king simply refused to believe her.

Husn Bano tried to prove her point by calling her nurse as a witness. But the king, because of his blind faith in the holy man, did not believe Husn Bano.

He got so annoyed with Husn Bano that he decided to punish her. He took away her palace and ordered her to get out of the kingdom along with her old nurse.

She and her nurse were turned out of their palace without any food or money.

They were left by the guards in the forest. They did not know what to do or where to go, as they had never been to the forest alone.

The two women were terrified on hearing the ferocious roars of animals in the dark and dense forest. But they decided to act bravely.

They decided to sleep by turns so that they could be safe in the forest. Husn Bano slept while her nurse kept guard.

While sleeping, Husn Bano saw a dream in which she saw an old man with a white beard.

The old man told her to dig the earth near the tree where she was lying asleep. He told her that there was treasure there and it was for her.

When she woke up, Husn Bano told the nurse about her dream .

Just then, she saw one of her old servants coming towards her. He had brought food for them. Husn Bano asked him to bring something to dig the ground.

Next day, the servant brought a spade. Then they quickly dug for the treasure and found it. It was just as Husn Bano had seen in her dream.

There was a lot of gold and money there. Husn Bano thanked God for giving her the wealth.

She then asked her old servant to arrange for people who could build houses and roads. She wanted to build a beautiful city in the same forest.

The servant told her that she would have to take permission from the king before building the city. So Husn Bano, dressed as a merchant, went to the king.

She introduced herself as Maaru Shah and asked the king to allow her to build a city in the forest.

The king not only allowed her to build the city, but also provided her help in building it.

When the city was complete, it looked wonderful. Husn Bano started living in a palace of her city.

MAARU SHAH

One day Husn Bano, disguised as Maaru Shah, went to see the king.

The king told her that he was going to meet a holy man.

Husn Bano, dressed as Maaru Shah, asked the king if she could accompany him. The king agreed, and then both of them went to meet the holy man. He was the same man who had stolen her wealth.

While returning, she told the king that she wanted to call the holy man for dinner.

As her city was far away, she requested the king to allow her to use a small palace where she could call the holy man.

The palace given to her was the one where she used to live earlier.

The king got the small palace cleaned up, and dinner was prepared for the holy man and his students.

When the holy man came, he and his students were given a sumptuous meal.

Husn Bano knew what the holy man would do at night. So she sent a message to the king asking him to send a few of his soldiers to the palace, on the pretext that she needed them to guard the palace.

As was expected, the robbers came at night and began stealing the wealth that was there in the palace.

The king's soldiers saw the robbers stealing and caught them red-handed.

The king was furious when he came to know that the holy man was caught by his soldiers.

He angrily told his soldiers, "Under my rule no holy man shall ever be mistreated. Leave the holy man and his students immediately, or I'll throw all of you out of my kingdom, as I threw Husn Bano."

Then Husn Bano, dressed as Maaru Shah, came to meet him and told him that this holy man was actually a robber.

The king believed her this time because she had sufficient evidence to prove it. Moreover, the king's soldiers had caught him red-handed.

All the forty robbers, along with their chief, were hanged on the king's order.

The king sadly told Maaru Shah that Husn Bano, his dear friend's daughter, had also told him about the holy man, but he had not believed her and had turned her out of her palace.

The king felt very apologetic about his behaviour towards Husn Bano. He told Maaru Shah, "I have ill-treated my friend's daughter. How will I ever amend for what I did to Husn Bano?"

Maaru Shah then took off her disguise, and the king saw that it was Husn Bano herself.

The king was extremely happy to see her safe and unharmed.

She told him about the treasure she had found and the palace where she lived.

The king went with Husn Bano to her city and happily spent few days there. He then left her in her wonderful city and came back to his palace.

"That is all I know about Husn Bano. The city I went to was the city made by Husn Bano herself," said Muneer.

Then Muneer again expressed his desire to marry Husn Bano.

Hatim assured Muneer, "Muneer Shah, I will see to it that you get married to Husn Bano. I will go and meet her, and I shall convince her to marry you after solving the seven puzzles set by her."

Muneer thanked Hatim for his kindness and told him the way to Husn Bano's city.

HATIM TAKES OVER

Hatimtai told his ministers that he would be away for sometime. He asked them to manage the kingdom with the help of Prince Muneer, who'll stay in the palace till he returns.

So Hatim set out on the journey to fulfill his promise. The first thing he did was to meet Husn Bano.

He talked to her while she sat behind a curtain.

Hatim said, "I will try and solve all the seven puzzles you have asked."

Husn Bano said, "Why are you doing all this?"

Hatim said, "I am not doing this for myself. After I solve all the seven puzzles, you will have to marry the man whom I want you to."

Husn Bano agreed and told Hatim about the first puzzle. He had to find out who said these words and why, '*Have seen it once but would like to see it again.*'

THE ADVENTURE BEGINS

Hatimtai did not know how he should start looking for the answer to the first puzzle. So he kept on walking.

One day, while walking through a forest he saw a wolf hunting a deer. The deer was running as fast as it could to save itself.

Just when the wolf was about to catch the deer, Hatim ran and stopped him. The deer ran away.

The wolf spoke in a man's voice and said, "Hatimtai you might be very kind, but you have not been fair to me."

"Why? How have I been unfair to you?" asked Hatim.

"You saved the deer but don't you see, you have left me hungry. What will I eat now? The pangs of hunger are killing me," said the wolf.

Hatim realised that the wolf was right in accusing him. So he decided to make up for his mistake by giving his flesh to the wolf.

He said, "You will not go hungry. I have deprived you of your food, so I'll substitute for it."

Hatim cut off some flesh from one of his leg and gave it to the wolf to eat.

The wolf had tears in its eyes when it saw this. It said, "I had heard a lot of your kindness, but you have proved yourself to be greater than my expectations."

Hatim said, “I cannot see anyone hungry or in pain.”

The wolf said, “I want to help you Hatimtai. What brings you here to the forest?”

Hatim told the wolf the story of the seven puzzles of Husn Bano that he had to solve. When Hatim told her about the first puzzle, the wolf said that it knew where he could find the answer to this puzzle. It said, “You will find this in a far away land.”

The wolf gave him the directions. Hatim thanked him and set out again.

On the way, he felt a great pain in the leg where he had cut his flesh. He could not walk as the pain was too much for him to bear any further.

He groaned and fell down. A pair of jackals heard him and came to help him.

The wife of the jackal said, “We must help this man. He is the great Hatimtai.”

The jackal put some herbs on the wound because of which the wound soon got healed.

Hatim thanked them and said, “You have helped me. Is there anything I can do for you?”

The jackal said, "A lion couple always eats our babies. We'll be grateful if you could help us."

Hatim went straight to the caves of the lion couple to ask them not to kill the babies of any animal.

When Hatim asked the lion couple to be considerate towards the babies of other animals, they said, "We are the King and the Queen of the Forest. We can kill anyone. Today we will eat you."

The lion and the lioness pounced on Hatim. But brave as he was, he soon overpowered them and took out their nails and teeth.

When they cried in pain, Hatim prayed to God to lessen their pain.

The lion said, "You have taken out our nails and teeth. How will we hunt now? We will have to remain hungry and die."

The jackal came there and said, "I will bring food for you every day. You will not remain hungry."

On being sure of the well being of both the jackals and the lions, Hatim felt better and he resumed his journey.

HATIM'S BEAR WIFE

Hatimtai walked on, but he realised that he had lost his way. When he was thinking about which way to take, he saw two bears coming towards him.

They told him that the Bear King wanted to meet the great Hatimtai. So Hatim went with the bears to meet the Bear King.

The Bear King was very happy to see Hatim. He asked him to marry his bear daughter.

When Hatim refused to marry his daughter, the Bear King got very angry and offended. He ordered his bear soldiers to throw Hatim into a pit.

At night, Hatim saw a dream. In his dream, an old man with white hair told him to marry the Bear Princess as she would help him in his quest.

So the next day, Hatim went to the Bear King and told him that he was ready to marry his daughter.

Amidst a lot of celebrations by the bears, Hatimtai was married to the Bear Princess.

A few days after his marriage, Hatim felt guilty about taking so long in finding the answer of the first puzzle.

He told his bear wife to tell her father to let him go, as he had to fulfill the promise he had given to his friend.

Hatim was then allowed to go by the Bear King. His wife gave him a big jewel which she said would save him from danger.

Hatim kept the jewel in his turban and continued his journey. After walking for a few days, he found himself in a desert.

It was very hot, and he found it difficult to walk in the scorching heat of the sun. He also felt very hungry and thirsty.

Suddenly an old man with a white beard appeared with food and water. Hatim ate the food and felt better.

Then the white haired man vanished. Hatim thanked God for helping him and moved on.

All of a sudden, a very big snake came in front of him. The snake drew a deep breath, and the next moment Hatim found himself inside the snake.

He looked for his sword to cut the skin of the snake to get out of it, but the sword was left outside.

It was dirty inside the body of the snake. Hatim realised that the jewel of his bear wife was saving him, as he was alive even in the snake's body.

Hatim started running inside the huge snake trying to find some way out, but he couldn't.

He ran up and down for three days.

On the fourth day, the snake felt pain inside its stomach because of Hatim's running up and down. So it threw Hatim out of its stomach. Hatim was dirty, but alive.

After washing his clothes and having a bath, he felt better.

He walked on and came to a beautiful part of the forest from where he could see a mountain.

He started climbing the mountain. On the top of the mountain, he saw a house. He walked in and saw a bed there.

As he was very tired, he laid on the bed and went to sleep. When he got up, he saw a white haired man sitting near him.

Hatim told him his story and what he was looking for.

The old man warned him that whoever goes there never comes back.

However, Hatim boldly said, "I have to do this for a friend, no matter what the consequence is."

The old man said, "You are very brave and kind, so I will help you."

He told Hatim that he would meet some beautiful girls. They would take him to a beautiful woman who would solve the puzzle for him.

Hatim asked for the blessings of the old man. The old man blessed him and gave him a piece of wood.

"What is this?" asked Hatim.

The old man said, "If you keep it in your mouth, you will become invisible. No one will be able to see you. This magical piece of wood will help you in your quest."

Hatim thanked the old man for the gift and walked towards the direction told by him.

He soon reached a beautiful field. There he saw a lake of clear water.

As he roamed about, he saw some pretty girls. He then remembered what the old man had told him.

Hatim followed them and went into the pool of clear water. All of a sudden, he felt that he was going inside the water but to his own surprise he could still breathe.

HAVE SEEN IT ONCE AND WOULD LIKE TO SEE IT AGAIN

Hatim found himself in a very beautiful palace under the water. He entered its hall and saw a beautiful woman sitting on a golden throne.

He was so mesmerised by the beauty of the woman that he couldn't take his eyes off her. He had never seen such a beautiful woman in his life. A beauty that was unblemished and spotless!

He knew that he was in front of a Fairy Queen and all the others were also fairies.

Hatim walked up to the lovely Fairy Queen and held her hand.

Suddenly, everything disappeared. The palace was no longer there. There were neither any fairies nor any Fairy Queen around.

Hatim found himself in the middle of a wild land.

He suddenly heard a loud voice, "*Have seen it once and would like to see it again.*"

These were the very words of his first puzzle!

Hatim looked in the direction from where the voice was coming.

A man, with long hair and a long beard, was sitting on a nearby rock.

Hatim ran towards that man and asked him, "Why did you speak these words?"

The man asked, "Who are you?"

Then Hatim told him his story. He also told him about seeing the Fairy Queen.

The man said, “So you have been sent here by the lovely Fairy Queen. I too was sent here by her.”

“But why?” asked Hatim.

The man said, “I saw her and as she was so beautiful, I held her hand. So she sent me here.”

“She was so beautiful that even I couldn’t stop myself from holding her hand. But that was surely a mistake,” said Hatim.

“Her beauty was so mesmerising, I couldn’t help it. I have seen her once and want to see her again,” said the man.

Hatim thought of a solution and said, “Come with me. I will get you back to her, but this time don’t hold her hand.”

He took the man with him and tried to get back to the pool of water but could not do so.

Then he took out the piece of wood that the old man had given him. He put it in his mouth.

The man with him shouted, “Where are you, Hatim?” But Hatim did not reply.

He realised that the piece of wood had worked its magic; he had become invisible.

Hatim quickly found a shortcut to the pool. Then he went back to the place where he had left the man. He took out the piece of wood from his mouth and became visible again. Then Hatim brought the man to the pool. He left him there and hid himself.

He saw the fairies come and take the man into the pool. Hatim reminded him again not to touch the Fairy Queen and left the place.

He now felt that he should go back to Husn Bano and tell her that he had found the answer to the first puzzle.

It was a very long journey, but finally Hatim reached her palace.

Husn Bano was happy to know that Hatim had solved the first puzzle.

DO GOOD AND CAST IT INTO THE RIVER

Husn Bano told Hatimtai about the second puzzle, "You have to find out the man who has written this on the front wall of his house, '*Do good and cast it into the river.*'"

Husn Bano was so happy after having the first puzzle solved that she gave a hint to Hatim.

She told him that this man lived towards the north of her city.

Hatim began his search for this man. He went through many difficulties, but he bravely moved on.

After a long time, he reached a big palace. On its front wall was written, 'Do good and cast it into the river.'

Before walking inside the palace, Hatim put the piece of wood in his mouth as there were many soldiers guarding the palace. Now nobody could see him.

In the court, he saw a very old man sitting on the throne.

Hatim took out the piece of wood and met the old man, who welcomed Hatim and offered him food.

After having some food, Hatim asked the old man to explain the meaning of the words on the front wall of his beautiful palace.

The old man said that these lines were related to his own life's story.

Hatim said, "I would like to hear it."

The old man then told him his story. He said, "Hatimtai, you may not believe it, but when I was young, I was a thief."

"I was bad and cruel, but everything I did was not bad. The only good thing I did was to put two pieces of bread in the river every day, for the fishes to eat. Once I fell very ill and felt as if I was going to die."

"Then a messenger of death came to take me to hell. On the gates of hell, two angles appeared and they told the messenger of death that I was to be sent back to earth to live for a hundred more years."

"When I asked the angels why I was spared from going to hell, they told me that though I had done a lot of bad deeds, one good deed that I did every day saved me from being damned."

"When I opened my eyes, I saw that I was in my bed. The two bread pieces had become two angels who saved me from going to hell . Afterwards, I made it a habit to put two pieces of bread in the river every day. I put them and then forget about it. I forget about it but God doesn't. So as a reward, I get two hundred gold coins that come with the river water. With that money I help the poor people."

"I believe that we should be kind to everyone and then forget our good deeds. We should not ask for anything in return."

"This is the reason why I have got it written on the front wall of my palace, '*Do good and cast it into the river.*'"

Hatim thanked the old man and started his journey back to Husn Bano's city.

He had solved the second puzzle too and wanted to tell her.

On his way, he saw that a big black snake was about to eat a golden snake. He could not bear to see this. He took out his sword and killed the cruel black snake.

Suddenly the golden snake disappeared. Hatim looked around to see whether it had slithered behind the bushes.

Then all of a sudden, a young man appeared in the place where he had previously seen the golden snake. He was standing next to the dead black snake.

The young man said, "I am the Prince of Jinns. You have saved me from my slave."

"Do you mean that this black snake was your slave?" asked Hatim, pointing towards the dead snake in front of him.

"Yes, today he would have killed me had you not come to save me. Thank you so much," said the grateful young man.

Hatim said, "Don't thank me, thank the Lord that he sent me here at the right time to save you."

The young man said, "You must come with me to my kingdom."

He then took Hatim to his palace. There the King of Jinns thanked Hatim for saving his son. He gave him a lot of money and gifts, all of which Hatim gave to the poor.

The young Prince of Jinns said, "I know that you are brave, but if you ever need help just think of me. I will immediately come to help you."

The King of Jinns also gave a magic stick and a magic jewel to Hatim as a gift.

The magic stick would become a boat when thrown into water, and the magic jewel had the power to cure the bite of poisonous snakes.

Before Hatim went away, the king bade him farewell and said, "I am glad to meet you. You are courageous and tender-hearted, a rare combination of qualities."

Hatim thanked the father and the son and moved on his way to the city of Husn Bano.

Hatim reached her palace and told her that he had solved the second puzzle too. She was glad to hear of it.

EVIL BEGETS EVIL

Husn Bano then told Hatimtai about the third puzzle, "In the forest, you will find a man saying that *Evil begets Evil*. You have to find the meaning of these words."

Hatim immediately set off to solve the third puzzle. He walked for many days till he came near a mountain. A very weak young man was sitting there and was crying aloud, “Come back to me!”

Hatim went and asked the man, "Why are you crying like this?"

The man said, "I am a merchant. When I was going through this way, I saw a beautiful lady. An exquisite beauty, indeed! I fell in love with her the moment I saw her. I told her that I wanted to marry her, and she agreed to marry me."

"If she agreed to marry you then what is the problem?" asked Hatim.

"I was very happy when she agreed, but then she said that she would like to meet her family before going with me. She went away and hasn't come back since then. I can't live without her," said the young man sadly.

Hatim asked the man to come with him, and they would search for her together .

The man said, "I cannot come with you. I cannot leave this place because she said that if I go away, I will never see her again."

Hatim said, "How long can you wait here?"

"Forever. I have been waiting here for the last seven years," said the man.

"Where does she live?" asked Hatim.

"She is a fairy. She lives on that mountain," said the man, pointing towards a far away mountain.

Hatim decided to go and meet the fairy. He climbed up the mountain and saw a lovely palace where many fairies were singing songs.

He asked them where he could find that fairy. They took him near another mountain.

There he saw another young man crying. Hatim asked him why he was crying.

The man told him that he was a soldier. He loved the daughter of a magician, but the magician had put some conditions for him to marry her.

The first condition was to get a pair of *pariru*. The second was to get a red snake's jewel. The third was to jump into a tank of hot boiling oil and come out without getting burnt.

The soldier said, "I can't do all this, yet I love her a lot. So I am just crying. What else can I do?"

Hatim said, "Don't worry. I will help you."

Hatim had a generous soul. He couldn't see anyone in pain. So he set out to fulfill the three conditions that could get the soldier, the girl he dearly loved.

The first condition was to get a pair of *pariru*. He knew that a *pariru* was a peacock with a human face.

He reached a moated town. A moat is a ditch made around a city to prevent enemies from coming in.

All the people of the city were sitting together, as if discussing something. Dejection and gloom was clearly evident on their faces.

Hatim asked one of them, "Why are you all so sad? What is the matter?"

The man said, "A demon troubles us every night. He comes and kills five or six of us every night."

Hatim decided to help them.

Hatim saw fear in the eyes of these people. Instead of happily playing in the open fields of the city, the children were locked up inside the houses for the fear of the demon.

Hatim wanted to stop the demon from brutally killing these innocent people. He made a plan to stop the demon from coming to that city.

He told the people to fill the moat with logs and put it on fire when the demon comes at night.

All the people of the town worked according to Hatim's plan, hoping that this God sent man would save them from this demon.

In the evening when they were waiting for the demon to come, Hatim saw a huge figure with seven heads. Each head had one huge eye. This was the demon.

As soon as he came near the moat, Hatim told the people to put the logs on fire.

Seeing the huge flames of fire, the demon moved backwards.

Just then Hatim hit an arrow at him which pierced his middle eye. Groaning with pain, the demon ran away into the forest in which he lived.

The people of the city heartily thanked Hatim. The king of that city gave him many gifts, all of which he gave to the needy.

Then Hatim resumed his search for a pair of *pariru*. After crossing a river, with the help of the magic stick given by the King of Jinns, he saw many *parirus*. When he told them his story, two *parirus* agreed to come with him. Hatim gave the *parirus* to the soldier, who took them to the magician.

After this Hatim went in search of the red snake's jewel. He reached a desert where he got to a hot mountain. The mountain was so hot and Hatim so tired that he fainted.

Suddenly, he heard a voice say, "Now use the magic jewel."

When he opened his eyes, he saw a huge red snake coming towards him. Fire was coming out from the snake's mouth. Hatim knew that this was the snake whose jewel had to be obtained.

So, he threw his magic jewel at the snake. The snake got scared and threw out a jewel. Hatim quickly picked it up and took it to the young soldier. The soldier went to the magician and gave the jewel to him.

The third thing had to be done now. The soldier had to jump into a tank full of hot boiling oil and come out of it without getting burnt.

Hatim gave the soldier the jewel given by his bear wife and told him that it would protect him when he jumps into the tank of hot boiling oil.

The soldier kept the jewel in his mouth and jumped into the tank of hot boiling oil.

He came out of it without getting burnt.

When the soldier came out of the tank, he hugged Hatim. His eyes were full of gratitude for him.

The happy magician organised a grand ceremony for the wedding of his daughter to the soldier.

Hatim blessed the soldier and his wife, and then went on his way.

Now he had to convince the fairy to marry the young man who had been waiting for her for seven long years.

He reached the mountain where he was told he would find the fairy. When he went inside the cave of the mountain, he saw a palace.

Many fairies came and stood around Hatim.

One asked, "Who are you?"

Hatim replied, "I am Hatimtai. I am the King of Yemen."

Another asked, "Why have you come here?"

Hatim said, "I am looking for the fairy who is the beloved of a young man who has been waiting for her for the past seven years."

He was taken to that fairy but she said, "I have nothing to do with that young man."

That night when he fell asleep, he saw the white haired man again.

He told Hatim, "Tell the young man to put the jewel given by your bear wife in his mouth. Then let him drink half a glass of milk. Give the rest of the milk to this fairy to drink. Once she drinks that milk, she will start loving the man."

When Hatim woke up, he requested the fairy to call the young man to her palace.

When the young man came, Hatim gave the jewel of his bear wife to him. He asked him to keep the jewel in his mouth and drink half a glass of milk. The young man did as he was told. Hatim gave the rest of the milk to the fairy.

The moment the fairy drank the milk, she fell in love with the young man.

She said, "I am sorry for causing you so much pain and trouble. Please forgive me. I love you, and I wish to marry you."

The fairy and the young man were married amidst a lot of celebrations.

Hatim moved on to solve the third puzzle of Husn Bano. He didn't know where he should go.

Then he thought, "The Prince of Jinns could help me with this."

He thought of the prince, and the young prince came and stood in front of him.

The prince happily greeted Hatimtai and asked him, "How can I help you, Hatim?"

Hatim told him about the third puzzle which asked him to find out the meaning of the words, 'Evil begets Evil.'

The prince then closed his eyes and meditated for sometime. He opened his eyes and said, "I think I can tell you where you should go."

The prince explained the way but then he said, "It is very far. It will take you months to reach that place. Take this magic carpet. With its help you will reach there soon."

Hatim took the magic carpet and thanked the prince for his help.

He unfolded the carpet and stood on it. Slowly, the magic carpet went flying in the air. He took the way that the Prince of Jinns had told him.

On reaching his destination, he saw a cage hanging on a tree. The cage had an old blind man in it.

He went towards the cage and asked the blind man, "Who has put you in this cage?"

"I am here because of my own mistake. No one else is responsible for my condition," said the blind old man gloomily.

"First let me get you out of this cage, then tell me your story," said Hatim.

"No! One thing has to be done before I come out of this cage," said the blind old man.

"What is it?" asked Hatim.

"Hear my story, and you will know what it is," said the blind old man.

He began, "I was a merchant. My father died and left a lot of money for me, but I wasted all the money in having fun. When my father's money was finished, I needed more money."

"I had always known that my father had buried a lot of wealth under our house. I tried to find out someone who was good at finding hidden treasures by knowing where exactly to dig."

"I found such a man. I told him that I would give him a part of the buried wealth, if he found it."

"The young man found the buried wealth. But I, due to my greed, refused to give him anything."

"Instead, I beat him up and threw him out of my house. I was blind with greed!"

"After a few days, I met the young man again. Surprisingly, he was still friendly towards me. He proposed to teach me, how to find buried treasures. He said that he would put a magic lotion on my eyes which would enable me to see hidden treasures. But when he applied that lotion, I became blind."

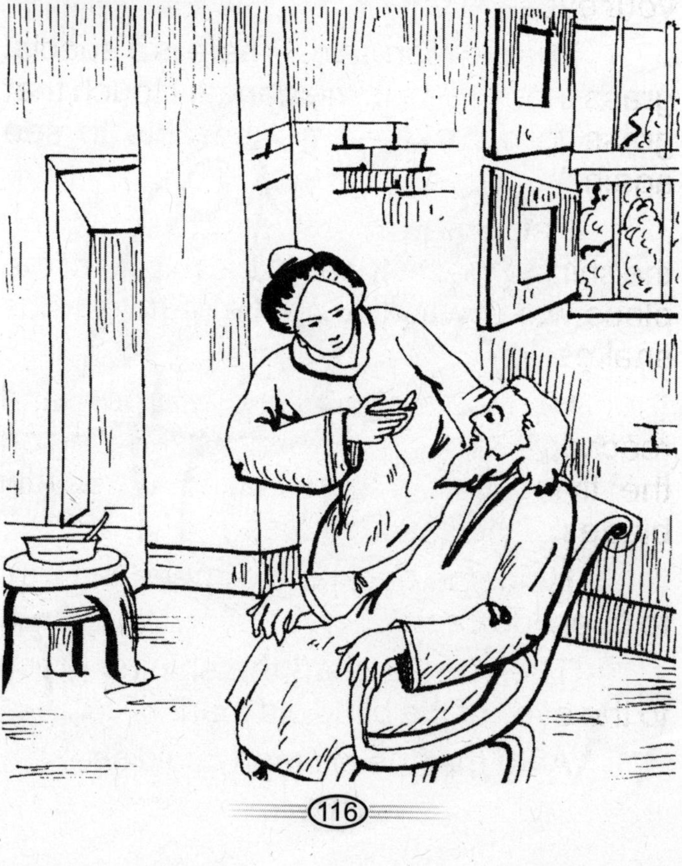

"The man had taken his revenge."

"After that he put me in this cage and hung me here. So I always say that ***Evil begets Evil***."

"I am waiting for my eyesight to come back."

Hatim asked, "How can you get your eyesight back?"

The old man said, "There is a special grass that shines in the dark. If I touch that grass to my eyes, I will be able to see again."

Hatim was told where he could find the shining grass. It was in the middle of the place which was the abode of poisonous snakes.

He took the flying carpet and reached that place. He bent while sitting on the flying carpet and picked up a few blades of the shining grass.

He came back and climbed the tree to open the cage.

Then he touched the shining grass to the eyes of the blind old man.

After that the old man could see.

Hatim helped him to climb down the tree. The old man was grateful to Hatim for what he had done.

Husn Bano jumped with joy when Hatim told her that he had successfully solved the third puzzle .

PLEASURE LIES IN SPEAKING THE TRUTH

Hatimtai did not want to waste any time. So he asked Husn Bano to tell him about the next puzzle. Husn Bano said, "The fourth puzzle is to find out the mystery behind the words, '*Pleasure lies in speaking the truth.*'"

Husn Bano was so happy with Hatim that she even told him the city where he would find the answer to this puzzle.

Hatim started on his journey again. Since he knew his destination, he hoped that he would soon solve the puzzle.

It was not an easy journey. After facing a lot of hardships, he managed to reach the city that Husn Bano had told him about.

There he walked around the city looking for the house where the mystery of the puzzle could be solved.

After a long time, Hatim reached a big house on whose walls it was written, *Pleasure lies in speaking the truth.*

Hatim asked the servant outside about the owner of the house.

He was told that the old man was eight hundred years old and so was the city in which he lived.

He asked the servant to inform the owner that he, Hatimtai, wanted to meet him.

When he was taken inside, Hatim asked the old man why the words, 'Pleasure lies in speaking the truth,' were written on the wall of his house.

In reply, the old man told him his story.

This man had been a gambler and had lost all his money in gambling. One day when he needed money, he stole the king's necklace while the king was fast asleep in his palace. When he was running away, he met two thieves who stopped him, intending to rob him.

The thieves tried to snatch the necklace from the gambler. They started beating him when he resisted.

Then suddenly a strange looking man came to help the gambler. He used his magical powers to rescue him from the thieves.

The thieves got scared and ran away, leaving the necklace.

The gambler thanked the strange looking man for saving him.

The man told the gambler that he had come to help him because of some good deeds he had done in his life.

He said, “You can keep the necklace with you. If you promise that you will never gamble again, you will live for nine hundred years as the king of a city.” Saying this, the strange man suddenly disappeared.

After this incident, the gambler stopped gambling and started leading a truthful life.

He made a huge house for himself and lived there. The people who were jealous of him went to the king and asked him to inquire into the source of his wealth.

The king called the man and asked him about his wealth. The man told the truth to the king.

The king was so impressed that instead of punishing him for stealing the necklace, he rewarded him and made him the king of the city he was living in.

This was the reason why the man had got it written on the wall of his house that ***Pleasure lies in speaking the truth***.

In this way, Hatim solved the fourth puzzle.

He went back to Husn Bano to tell her about it. She was overjoyed at Hatim's success and admired his courage and intelligence.

THE ECHOING MOUNTAIN

Husn Bano then told Hatim about the next puzzle. She said, "You have to go and get information about a mountain that echoes. Find out what the echo of the mountain signifies."

Hatim reached a town and met the head of the town.

The head knew in which kingdom he could find the mountain that echoed. He gave Hatim the direction to that kingdom.

When Hatim reached there, he asked some guards to take him to the king.

On meeting the king, Hatim said, "I am Hatimtai, the King of Yemen. I want to know about the echoing mountain."

The king asked him to stay in his kingdom for a few days to know about the echoing mountain.

One day, when the king was having lunch with Hatim, they heard a strange voice calling, "Come quickly, come quickly."

They looked out of the window and saw a man running towards the direction from where the voice was coming. His face was red and was getting redder.

Other people were trying to stop him, but the man shook them off and ran ahead.

The king told Hatim that this voice was the echo of the mountain.

Hatim ran after the man.

Just when Hatim came near the mountain, the mountain and the man both disappeared. Hatim returned from the mountain sadly.

During the next few days, he saw many people running towards the mountain and disappearing.

Hatim befriended a nice young man in the town. Both of them liked each other a lot. They spent much time with each other.

He told Hatim that once the voice of the mountain summons a person, he or she has to follow its order. He also told him that whoever follows its echo never returns.

One day when Hatim and his friend were sitting together, the mountain echoed. Hatim's friend started running towards the mountain.

Hatim ran after him and caught his friend's hand. Both of them ran together.

They climbed the mountain. On the top of the mountain was a fort.

As they came near the fort, Hatim stepped on the grass but his friend put his foot on the stone floor.

The man fell down and died. Hatim understood that the echo of the mountain was the call of death.

This was the way that the people of this city died when their time came.

Hatim thought that now he could go to Husn Bano and tell her the mystery of the echoing mountain.

Hatim tried to find his way back, but he got lost. Then he put the magic piece of wood in his mouth and climbed down the mountain.

On his way back, he saw a river. There was a boat in the river. Hatim sat in it and started rowing.

He got down on the other side and walked on. After sometime, he saw a river that had red water. The water was blood red, but Hatim was able to cross the river safely.

Then he saw another river which had silver water. He put his hand in it, and it became silver.

Then he came to a river that had clear water in it. He put his silver hand in the water of this river, and his hand turned normal again.

Then he saw a river of fire. Huge flames of fire were coming out of this river.

He kept the jewel, given by his bear wife, in his mouth and safely crossed the river of fire.

Finally, he reached the palace of Husn Bano and told her how he had solved the fifth puzzle.

THE QUEST FOR THE PEARL

Hatimtai told Husn Bano, “Now please tell me the sixth puzzle that I have to solve. My friend must be waiting for me.”

Husn Bano said, “This time you have to get the pearl which is of the same size as a duck’s egg. I have one like that with me.”

Husn Bano showed the pearl to Hatim. He said, “Please make a copy of this in silver, so that I bring the right sized pearl.”

Husn Bano gave a silver replica of the pearl to Hatim, and he began his journey to solve the sixth puzzle.

He could not think of any place to start looking for the pearl. So he sat down and wondered what to do. He thought of the magical things he had.

Then an idea struck him. He thought he would put the magic piece of wood between his teeth and see if it helped him.

He put the magic piece of wood between his teeth, and suddenly he started hearing many voices around him.

He could hear many things at a time. Trees were talking to each other, and animals were calling each other.

Then he heard a voice above him. He saw two birds, with white and red feathers, sitting on the branch of the tree above him.

He heard a sweet bird asking, “Who is this man?”

The male bird told the female bird, “This man is Hatimtai. He is the brave and strong King of Yemen. He has left his kingdom and is solving the seven puzzles set by Husn Bano for his friend, Muneer Shah. He has already solved five puzzles.”

“Which puzzle is he to solve this time?” asked the female bird.

The male bird told her, “Husn Bano has asked him to get a pearl of the size of a duck’s egg. But those pearls are not found now.”

“If those pearls are not found now, how will this poor man find it?” asked the female bird.

“There are only two such pearls to be found now. One is with Husn Bano. She found it when her servants were digging the earth to build her city,” told the male bird.

“If one of the two pearls is with Husn Bano, where is the other pearl?” asked the female bird.

The male bird said, “There was a queen who found this while she was sitting near a river. That queen had lost her husband in a war and was going to have a baby soon. A merchant took her home and took care of the queen like his own daughter. She gave birth to a son who later became a king. Now his family has the pearl. The king has decided that he would give the pearl and marry his daughter to the man who would tell him where the huge pearl came from.”

“But how will this man reach that kingdom? I have heard that there are many demons and giants over there,” said the female bird.

The male bird said, “If he takes our red feathers, dips them in water and sprays the water on himself, he can change his form.”

“But how will he remain safe?” asked the female bird.

The male bird said, “If he sprays water on his face with our white feathers, he will be safe. Afterwards, he can come back to his normal form by taking a bath.”

When the birds flew off some of their feathers dropped on the ground near Hatim. Hatim quickly picked up the feathers and did as the birds had said.

Then he began his journey. On his way, he saw a snake entering the nearby bushes. But instead of a snake, a young man came out of the bushes.

The young man happily and excitedly walked towards Hatim and introduced himself.

He said, "I am a prince. I was cursed by a witch to become a snake."

"How did you become a prince again?" asked Hatim.

The young man said, "I regained my original form only because of you. I was told that if an honest man comes near me, I would become a prince again. Many men have been near me, but only your presence could free me from the curse."

"I am glad I could help you," said Hatim.

"I want to help you too. What can I do for you?" asked the prince.

"Just tell me the way I should take to reach the place where there's a pearl of the size of a duck's egg," asked Hatim.

The prince said, "I will take you there in a flying machine. Sitting in it, you can go wherever you want in a short span of time."

The young man took Hatim to the flying machine and asked him to sit in it.

While going in the flying machine, Hatim saw a young man sadly wandering in the forest below.

Hatim asked the prince to stop the flying machine. They got down from the machine and went to the young man.

The compassionate Hatim asked the young man, "What is the matter? Why are you sadly wandering in this dangerous forest?"

"I am a prince, and I did not know where the pearl of the size of a duck's egg came from. So the king did not let me marry his daughter. I am sad because I cannot marry the princess. I can't even forget her because I really love her," said the young man.

Hatim assured him that he would get the woman he loved. He said, "Don't be sad, brother. I'll certainly help you in getting the woman you love."

He took the prince on the flying machine, and they reached the island.

When they walked into the palace, the king, on seeing the prince, angrily shouted, "Why have you come back?"

The prince said, "I have come with Hatimtai."

The king welcomed Hatim, who took out the silver replica of the pearl.

Hatim said to the king, "I wish to take the pearl you have."

The king said, "First you will have to tell me the story of the pearl. From where did this pearl come to me? If you tell me the story, you can get the pearl and even marry my daughter."

Hatim repeated all that he had heard from the birds.

The king was surprised to know that Hatim knew all the details about the pearl. The king then gave the pearl to Hatim.

The king's daughter was married to the prince who loved her a lot.

Hatim wished the prince and the princess a happy married life and began his journey back towards the city of Husn Bano.

He reached her city and went to meet her at her palace.

Husn Bano was delighted when Hatim gave her the pearl.

HAMMAM BAADGARD

Hatimtai then asked about the seventh puzzle.

Husn Bano said, “You have to find out the mystery behind the water in the Hammam Baadgard.”

“What do you want me to find out?” asked Hatim.

Husn Bano said, "Find out why the people who go there never come back alive? I'll give you a hint. Go to the south-west of my city."

On his way, he met an old man. When Hatim told him about his quest and that it was related to Hammam Baadgard, the old man said, "Son, it won't be easy to solve this puzzle."

The old man helped him by telling him how to reach the place.

Hatim journeyed for many weeks and reached a city. There he saw that some young girls were getting ready as brides. But the people were not happy there.

When Hatim asked them why they were all sad, he was told that a serpent was going to choose a bride for himself among these young girls.

The king said, "The serpent is a dangerously wicked *jinn.* We do not know how to save our daughters from him."

Hatim thought of a plan to save them.

When the serpent came, the king said, "Before you take any girl you must take permission from the true master of my city who has just arrived."

When the serpent met Hatim, he gave him some water to drink. In the water, Hatim had dipped the jewel given by his bear wife. The serpent drank it and died.

Everyone was happy and relieved because now they would not have to fear the wicked *jinn,* and now their daughters would be safe.

The king gave gold coins to Hatim as a reward, but he gave it to the poor and the needy people of the city.

Then Hatim resumed his journey. After travelling through many dangerous forests and encountering several wild creatures, he finally reached a mountain.

On climbing the mountain, Hatim found huge lizards and scorpions all around. He threw the magic jewel on the ground. As a result, all the lizards and scorpions began fighting amongst each other and eventually ate each other up. In this way, all of them died.

When Hatim reached the next city, the people were surprised to see him. He was the first traveller who had come to their city alive. He then told them how all the huge lizards and scorpions had died.

The king thanked Hatim because now no one would be afraid to cross the mountain to travel to other lands.

Hatim further travelled and reached another city. The king of that city asked Hatim to stay in his palace for some days.

Hatim agreed, as months of travelling had made him physically tired. The king and he became good friends.

When Hatim told the king about the seventh puzzle, he told him the way to reach Hammam Baadgard. The king told Hatim that whoever goes there never returns, but Hatim was undeterred by it.

The king gave him a letter for the gatekeeper of Hammam Baadgard, instructing him to help Hatim.

After a long journey, Hatim reached the gates of Hammam Baadgard.

When he gave the letter to the gatekeeper, he said, "Please don't go inside. No man has ever come out alive from here."

When Hatim insisted on going inside, the gatekeeper opened the gate.

On entering, Hatim saw another gate.

On it was written: *This is a magic house. Whoever comes here never goes out alive. If the time of his death has not come, he will have to live as a serpent here. But he cannot leave this magic house*.

Hatim went ahead. But when he turned back, he saw that there was no gate or gatekeeper. Then he saw a man coming towards him. The man said, “Come with me. I take newcomers for a bath.”

He took Hatim to a big tank of water. When Hatim went into the tank, the man disappeared.

Suddenly, the water started rising. Hatim saw an iron chain above the water.

He caught it and tried to climb it. Then came a loud noise, and he fell down.

When he opened his eyes, he found himself in a lovely garden. The garden was very beautiful, but there was a deadly silence in it; an eerie quietness.

He saw a man, but when he went closer, he realised that it was not a man but a stone statue. He saw many such stone statues in the garden.

Then he saw a parrot in a cage that was hung from a branch of a tree.

On a nearby wall, it was written: *No one goes from here alive because of a magic spell. This magic city was made by a magician who found a very big diamond here. He made this parrot eat the diamond. Anyone who kills the parrot will get the diamond. The magic spell will be broken, and the man can go home safely. There are three arrows kept here. If even one hits the parrot, the man will get the diamond, or else he will be turned into a stone statue.*

Hatim picked up the bow and the three arrows. He tried but failed to hit the parrot with the first two arrows.

Then he took the name of God and shot the third arrow. The third arrow hit the parrot. The diamond came out of the parrot's mouth and it died.

As soon as the parrot died, the spell of the magic house broke and everything changed.

The garden disappeared. The stone statues changed into living men, who came and thanked Hatim for freeing them from the evil magic spell.

When Hatim came outside, the gatekeeper was very happy to see him.

Hatim gave the diamond to his king friend, but the king gave it back to him saying that he should give it to Husn Bano as a proof that he had gone inside the Hammam Baadgard.

Hatim took leave of the king and went to the city of Husn Bano.

He told her the secret of Hammam Baadgard and presented her the big diamond.

Then Hatim said, "All the seven puzzles have been solved. Now you must do what I say."

"Yes, tell me what you want me to do?" asked Husn Bano.

"I want you to marry Muneer Shah. He is the Prince of Sham," said Hatim.

Husn Bano happily agreed to her marriage with Muneer Shah.

Husn Bano and Muneer Shah were married, and everyone celebrated their wedding day with great happiness.

When it was time to go with Muneer, Husn Bano cried as she bade goodbye to her nurse.

Muneer Shah and Husn Bano took Hatim with them to their kingdom. They requested him to stay with them for sometime. Hatim agreed and went with them.

Hatim was glad to see that Muneer and Husn were happy together.

HATIM'S MARRIAGE

One day Hatim took his leave from Husn and Muneer. He said, "It has been a long time since I have been away from my kingdom."

"Yes, you have taken ten years, seven months and nine days to solve the seven puzzles," said Husn Bano.

Muneer said, "I don't know how you did it so soon. Even a lifetime was less for it. They were not easy puzzles at all. Thank you for being so kind to us. You have faced so many dangers just to get both of us together."

Husn Bano told Hatim, "Muneer and I will never forget what you have done for us."

Hatim blessed both of them and went back to his own kingdom.

Everyone in his kingdom was overjoyed to see him back.

The ministers were happy to handover the kingdom back to Hatimtai.

All his six thousand brothers came to meet him. There was joy and happiness everywhere.

They told him that a fairy princess was waiting for him; she wanted to marry him as she was charmed by his courage and kind-heartedness.

When Hatim met the fairy princess, he was enchanted by her beauty. They spent much time in each other's company.

After spending sometime with each other, the fairy princess expressed her love for him. Even Hatim confessed that he loved her. But Hatim had not forgotten about his promise to his bear wife. He had to go back to her.

He told the fairy princess all about his bear wife and the jewel she had given him. He took her leave and went to his bear wife.

When he met her, he thanked her for the jewel she had given him. He told her how the jewel had kept him safe throughout his adventures.

He asked his bear wife to come to his palace to stay with him, but she refused. She told him that she had married him because she had wanted to help him in his quest.

She also said that he was free to marry whoever he wanted to, as she wanted to stay with her bear family.

Hatim went back to his kingdom and married the fairy princess. The wedding was celebrated according to the customs of the family.

There was a grand feast, and everyone blessed Hatim and his beautiful wife.

The King and the Queen of Yemen were kind and looked after their people very well.

God had blessed Hatim with a fearless soul. He was not only tender-hearted and generous, but also brave and heroic; indeed a rare combination of qualities.